More Tales
from an
Irish Hermitage

More Tales from an Irish Hermitage

Proceeds from this book go to feed the hungry and clothe the naked. We thank you for your purchase.

To see some of our other products, go to www.xanga.com/sistersofgraceofchrist

ISBN: 978-0-9809317-2-3

More Tales
from an
Irish Hermitage

by a Nun of Grace

Table of Contents

Introduction   1

Chapter One   5
    The Homing of Hunter-Cat   10

Chapter Two   36
    The Tale of the Wagtails   38

Chapter Three   46
    A Rooster called Rooney   47

Chapter Four   70
    Dilly, Dolly and Dally,
      the Hermitage Ducks
      (not forgetting Sir Francis...)   73

Chapter Five   102
    A Goat called Blossom   104

Chapter Six   130
    The Thursday Lamb   131

Postscript   144

Introduction...

Nestling into the green-shawled breast of an Irish mountain a small hermitage hides...

Reached only by a bridge, it is girded on the other three sides by water...two fast-flowing streams and the wide, restless sea...

Trees shelter it lovingly... old native ash and alder, rowan and willow.

Hawthorn and fuchsia hedge it...

Here dwells a Nun, a Monastic Solitary, living apart from her Order in a work of Cloistered Prayer.

Sister wears the full, traditional Monastic Habit of her Order.

Full-length, black habit, deep blue scapular, white guimp and large white wimple.

Her veil is long, deep blue lined with white.

In these modest garments, she is known and visibly a Nun.

The skills of her hands in her seclusion support the care of the homeless, especially children, in many lands where her Sisters in Christ Jesus live out their calling among the most needy of mankind

Her outgoings are few, for essentials only, her visitors fewer.

Her love for others expressed in her separation...

Hers are the seasons, the flowers and food she tends in her gardens... the wild flowers....

Hers the first birdsong of the day, the last sweet vespers they linger in...

Hers too are the creatures who enrich her life....

Those no one wants, like the little children her Sisters care for... the lost, the sick, the crippled, the rejected...

These tales are random... single threads in a rich tapestry of many years, taken from the pattern...

Single flowers in a fair posy...

They carry truth in them..

Inevitably then there is some overlapping, for lives intertwine always...

Beginnings and endings... Endings and beginnings...

Partings and meetings...

Chapter One

"Oh CAT!"

Sister dropped her knitting, as her jaw, as the saying goes, dropped in sympathy, seeing Caro stroll nonchalantly in through the wide open door.

"Oh CAT! Where have you been?"

And she hastily put the pale lemon wool well out of reach as the cat approached her.

The large, long-haired black and white cat was covered from the waist down with thick, black mud.

Not just wet, but caked in it.

And he cared not a whisker as he leapt gracefully onto Sister's lap... indignant then at being repelled so utterly swiftly.

Landing inelegantly afloor.

"What have you been doing?" Sister admonished, as the big cat gazed reproachfully, golden- eyed, up at her from the worn flagstones.

Never had she seen such mud; thick, black, viscous.

Amanda, usually eager to groom her twin, took one tentative lick, then stalked off in such clear disgust that Sister laughed aloud.

"Wise cat! But what to do now? He will never get that stuff off by himself..."

Maybe he had fallen in the ditch and only just managed to scramble out.

Sister blenched at the thought of this beloved animal sinking deeper and deeper and deeper into thick mire...until finally...

She shook herself.

"OK, my friend. Bathtime for you."

She scooped him up before he could understand what she meant, and deposited him in the bathroom, closing the window firmly.

An essential, as one of Caro's favourite tricks was to open any window.

And she made her preparations, washing the mud off her hands in distaste.

It was already starting to go hard and rigid.

Pottery clay?

Hmmmm.

"Although I may as well not bother, as I am sure there will be more all over me before the next hour is up…"

The bathroom was white tiled, with white bath and clean, stone tiled floor.

Was...

It took three lots of warm water and liquid detergent, three long rinses of increasingly pale water - for the first had been black as night - to get Caro even remotely clean.

Oh, he was a perfect gentleman, who had never shown any aggression to her in his life, and he allowed Sister to hold his front legs in one hand as she soaped and rinsed with the other.

But as the minutes passed, he shook himself more and more, spraying and spattering black mud all over the whiteness.

And in that split second when Sister let go of him to grab the old towels she had ready...

Oh MY!

Did he have a good shake of his long hair then...

Sister had donned her oldest habit, thankfully, as she and the floor and the walls were soaked...

And he struggled against the towels, mewing more and more loudly... until finally Sister gently helped him out through the window to dry off in the warm sun.

Then to clean the mess! And what a mess it was.

And her thoughts ranged far as she methodically washed and polished...

To other cats who had graced her life...

The Homing of Hunter Cat...

It was on an early June morning - early in June and early in the day - that Sister arrived at the Friary.

The hour was a glory of birdsong and blossom.

Laburnum trailed its fresh gold amid floating petals of cherry and almond.

The sea rippled gently in the freshness.

For, like most of the Friaries, this was set amid beauty.

Trees, mature forest, a sheltered sea estuary.

And beautiful, well-kept gardens all around.

It still lacked an hour to early Mass.

This was Sister's way, to be there in the dawning stillness, when Prayer is gentle and full.

When there is no one else there.

So she wandered a while in the quiet air.

Sat enthralled at the water's edge, watching sea birds diving for sand eels with unerring skill and accuracy.

Drama!

A keen, penetrating gaze as they cruised aloft, a pause and then - POUNCE.

Down like a sharp-tipped arrow into the water.

As Sister gentled silently past a flowerbed, movement caught her eye.

And she was startled and amazed to see three small kittens among the gaudy tulips.

Sweet tiny faces with huge eyes and large paws.

Gazing soulfully up at her, with pleading mews.

Sister crouched near them, moving slowly so as not to startle them.

But they came to her outstretched hand eagerly.

Her skilled gaze saw that their eyes still held some baby blue. So they were only a few weeks old.

A delicate shade of turquoise that would soon turn to gold or green.

Three pretty babies... Two tortie and one black.

Sister was mystified; but she knew hunger when she saw it.

There was, of course, cat food in the car...

For a cat lover never travels empty handed.

So she fetched a tin and pulled it open, spooning a little out onto a piece of paper.

And chuckled at the eager, "Yum, yum yums," of the trio.

And again at the "pecking order."

The bigger of the two torties holding down the head of the smaller one with an oversized paw until he had eaten his fill.

They were clearly used to being handled, so they were not ferals.

In any case, no feral cat would leave her babies in such an exposed place.

She stroked them gently, and they purred, and played with her fingers. Rolling over onto their backs, their full, furry tummies soft.

A voice behind her startled her.

There was a Diocesan Retreat in progress, and one of the priests was out for air before Mass.

And then, and after Mass, Sister learned that the trio had appeared the day before, apparently dumped there.

That made sense of their state, and of their amicable natures.

Clearly an unwanted litter, yet cared for until they could - just- eat by themselves.

Sister said nothing about the anger that these people simply did not care enough for cats to get them spayed.

It had after all been the same on the island, where cats were almost seem as vermin. They had no commercial value.

And, in a place where there had been great poverty, people thought it a waste to spend any money on them.

They begrudged it.

She had shamed a few there; and when she had still bred Siamese, had sold them for a good price. And seen and inwardly smiled at the reaction when folk learned of this.

And she knew that in Ireland there were groups striving to alleviate the problem of a large and often diseased feral cat population.

That when people moved house, they simply left the cats behind.

For she had fed them already often.

Inbred, weak, stunted creatures many of them.

So now she started pondering.

Her three cats, the last of her Siamese stock, were all elderly now.

All born of the same Siamese sire, but of different mothers.

All safely neutered at an early age.

And deeply attached to each other.

Sister knew that when one died, the others would soon follow.

Which would break her heart in many ways.

And so she had been wondering about a kitten; that would maybe become part of that family, and ease the times ahead.

And maybe rejuvenate the old ones!

But she had done nothing about it; simply waited and pondered.

And she watched and thought now.

After Mass, there were a number of priests around.

Sister smiled at their garb.

Some were in strict clerical black; but others wore soft collared tee or polo shirts in shades of sage or khaki.

The "uniform" off-duty wear that was as distinctive as their clericals.

And as she tended the babies, she learned that they had been there since the day before.

No-one, it seemed, had thought of feeding them.

Again, she said nothing.

So she determined now that she would ask if she could take one home; and maybe help find homes for the other two.

Knowing that if need be she would have to take all three; praying and hoping not.

As she was making that momentous decision, she saw the gardener approaching.

Carrying a cardboard box and wearing ridiculous thick gauntlets!

He would not look Sister in the eye, so she surmised that he was under orders to ... dispose of the kittens.

In a way that Sister would not approve...

He made a feeble excuse that the Friary had two dogs that would attack the kittens.

Sister knew the dogs; they were elderly and more feeble than this excuse.

She drew herself up to her full height - and Sister was not short - and told the man in no uncertain terms that if he harmed these little ones he would have her to answer to.

He was of middle age, so probably had been taught by ferocious Irish Sisters.

So her words counted to him.

She also made it easier for him by saying that if it would be allowed, she was happy to take one kitten.

And would help to find homes for the others...

(Although quite how she was going to do that she had no idea just then...)

But his face brightened then, as it "happened" that one of the cleaning ladies had said the same thing.

Sister uttered a silent prayer of thanksgiving.

She chuckled at his apprehension of the kittens, for he would not have handled them without protective gauntlets.

And she of course picked them all up easily and bare- handed.

Sure enough, the cleaning lady was ready to take the other two to her parish priest. He had demurred at three, but two would be fine.

So Sister chose the larger of the two torties. The other two would be happier with each other and she knew a "character" when she saw one.

And maybe he would need to be if her three acted up.

So into a cardboard box he went.

It was still early in the day, and sunny, so Sister lingered a while - especially as Father Guardian offered her good coffee and cakes at the café.

The Retreat Centre being full to bursting so that he could not offer her lunch.

So she played with her new baby on the grass by the sea.

Feeding him from her fingers.

An idyllic while indeed, for there are few things more charming than a small kitten.

Playing confidently in the warm sunshine.

He was a beauty.

A real charmer.

Who would have graced the lid of any chocolate box.

Soft, sweet face, huge eyes.

And with unusual markings.

For he had a large cross on his back, for all the world like an Irish donkey.

And a gentle, zany way with him.

Finally, wondering what her reception would be when she arrived home with the newcomer, she settled him in the box, carefully tied closed, and set off on the long drive home.

Baby- a temporary name until his true one became evident - however had different ideas.

Sister would drive a few miles - then be aware that a small, warm, furry body was climbing up the folds of her habit.

So she would stop, put him back in the box, tie it up again, and drive off again.

A kitten between hand and gear lever is not safe.

And is a great distraction at road junctions.

Thus it was that Sister drove home via a new and circuitous route; glorious scenery though...

Ireland in the sun; forested mountain slopes and deep, wide, shining lakes.

A beauty to linger in.

She realized that the kitten, taken too soon from his mother, was bonding strongly with her, adopting her as his mother.

Which was fine.

He needed to do that.

So she settled him on her lap safely; where he started to suck a bit of material for comfort.

Finally, Baby succumbed to sleep and the journey was accomplished successfully.

The cats came eagerly to meet her as she walked down the path - carrying the kitten of course.

Oh, SHOCK HORROR! WHAT IS THIS??

HOW DARE SHE DO THIS TO US?

Three pairs of outraged blue eyes
flashed ice at Sister.

And three expressive tails stalked away
disdainfully.

Sister was mortified.

The kitten clung to her, huge-eyed, and
so eager to leap down to play with these
other cats.

Restrained with great difficulty.

So the war began.

The long attrition of jealousy...

Sister did not sleep much that week.

Always a cat or two wanting to be where it did not want to find the intruder.

Hisses and spitting... snarling, growling.

So Baby had to sleep in the catbox in Sister's room; and the others thus could not sleep on her bed or even under it.

Total disruption.

Baby was a star; but Sister had also forgotten how much energy a small kitten had.

Needing to play and play and play.

Always of course with his new mother.

Trying to keep him away from the others was a nightmare; and he was such a friendly wee soul that he just could not understand why there was so much aggression to him.

He loved everyone.

And expected everyone to love him in return.

Was that not what life was all about?

It was out in the summer garden that the real fun began.

The three old ones loved to sleep on a blanket in the shade of a sycamore tree in the heat of the day.

All curled up together in complete oblivion and surrender.

Utterly peaceful; sprawled in total abandon.

Old ones, in their aged serenity.

To let them be in peace, Sister put Baby in the old hen coop for a wee while.

So that she and the cats knew where he was.

But he was so tiny and so determined to be friendly that he managed, while Sister was busy, to wriggle out through the mesh.

She came out of the door just in time to see, but not prevent, his enthusiastic, wholehearted leap on top of the trio.

WHOOSH!

SPLAT!

Utter outrage of old cats roused from sleep by this young hooligan.

Swearing and spitting, they abandoned the blanket and stalked off bog-eyed to try to find some peace.

While poor Baby was once more alone... he chased after them in vain.

Cats can vanish when cats need to vanish.

Time and time again, he leaped on them.

All he wanted was to play.

To wrestle as he had done with his siblings.

Time and time again, they spat at him and fled.

But he would not, or could not, take heed of the repulses.

Back he came; as if to say that, maybe this time it will be different.

It was weeks before even one of them calmed down and accepted the wee fellow.

Sister caught him licking the kitten...

Smiled and said nothing.

Lest he lose face for being seen to weaken.

And weeks more before the last of the three stopped spitting at him.

The first time Sister saw them all in a heap together, she prayed a deep thanksgiving.

He was utterly devoted to Sister, his new mother.

She was his lodestar, his sanctuary, the centre of his small world.

When she went down the path, he would follow; on the ground or up in the branches.

Always there where she was.

She would think she was alone, when suddenly he would land on her shoulders from a tree.

Purring and rubbing on her shoulder.

It was the year when the ewe lamb came, and the two grew up together. Rich games of hide and seek round the clumps of reeds.

Sister would take her knitting out to the back fence and work there, watching the two young critters play and race.

Zany clowns to enrich her life with laughter.

Then they would come to her, and curl up on her habit.

One on each side.

Purring and chewing the cud.

When she went to bed, there he would be, wriggling delightedly under the covers.

She stopped trying to prevent this.

May as well tell the sun not to shine.

And every day, because he had been taken from his mother far too soon, he would sit on her lap and suck any bit of cloth that was near, drooling heavily, eyes closed in utter bliss.

A habit that was to continue all his life long.

Sister never quite got used to the sodden patches on her habit or the bedclothes, and used to put a tissue under his mouth to catch the worst of the drips.

And all too soon, "Baby" grew up to earn his real name. Proved and earned - but not blooded.

For Sister chased him as he shot past with a wee critter in his jaws, and made him drop it.

Alive still.

That first time.

From then on, it was war of a different kind.

He would shoot past Sister at the door, and she would pause him with a quick hand. "Mouth empty, Hunter Cat?"

Sometimes it was; often it was not.

And in the latter case, the chase would be on.

And as he grew, the conflict between the two sides of his nature became more and more apparent - and it became more and more of a struggle for him to obey Sister and deny his hunting nature.

He was clearly torn between her and his deep instinct.

But always he was her devoted cat.

Always loving to all creatures of his own size.

When the pine marten came round, he would want to play and run with her.

To her horror of course.

Sister saw them sometimes in the summer dawn, racing and running together.

And once he came in with a bad badger bite on his back.

He had a way of finding trouble.

Once he went missing for three whole days.

Sister was demented.

Searching, calling, seeking.

Walking the land shouting his name.

Late one night, she thought she heard a weak cry from a thicket. She tore it apart, to no avail.

But later that night, in the deep, windless, wakeful silence, her keen, alert ears heard a faint, faint cry.

And there he was, under the window, too weak to climb.

Thin and haggard, and with a great lump on his jaw where clearly something had bitten him.

Sister deduced that he had got himself stuck in a rabbit hole, and had only managed to free himself when the weight had fallen off him.

But he never learned...

He was himself.

Through and through.

Chapter Two

Sister blinked and wiped her face with her capacious apron.

More than splashes from Caro's bath were there.

Hunter-cat was gone now...

And still she could not think of the way of that end.

Yet his sweet memory would never leave her.

His winning ways, and his deep affection. His many lives lost in escapades.

Until they were all used up.

Sister gave herself a good shake.

It was, she decided, time for a change in occupation now, after her unexpected toils.

The sun was shining, warm and full, so she set a chair out, made coffee, and took her knitting outside.

After changing her habit of course.

And hanging the old one out to dry.

The birds were out in force now, thronging the air with song and flight.

All old friends now.

And she smiled as the wagtails started their bobbing dance on the grass.

The Tale of the Wagtails...

The birds on the wooded shore
fascinated Sister.

She had once heard someone speak
disparagingly of British - and thus Irish
- birds, as being plain and dull and
dowdy.

Watching the life outside the Hermitage
windows as the news winged its way
around the feathered world that there
was food here, she saw, and heard, the
sweet variety of hue and song and shape.

Riches and fascination therein.

Nothing dull or plain, let alone dowdy.

Knowing the cats for the keen hunters
they were, Sister concocted a hanging
bird table.

For there had to be safety and a living
alongside in peaceful harmony.

It was very simple, as all good ideas are.

A piece of wood - part of an old
cupboard she found in the outbuilding.
Four cup hooks, and twine.

Cup hooks were indispensable, and
rarely used for cups.

A hook at each corner, a length of the strong blue bailer twine that was used for everything in these parts...

And the whole contraption carefully, delicately, painstakingly, suspended in the branches of the sycamore tree near the hermitage.

Carefully?

So that if anything heavier than a bird managed to touch it, as in a large furry predatory cat, the platform would tip and swing and refuse to be boarded.

It was ingenious - and it worked.

Hunter Cat tried once - and only once.

The indignity of being thrown off and having to scrabble at the tree trunk to try in vain to avoid a clumsy fall, was just too much.

So he, and the other cats, had to resort to... birdwatching.

As of course the birds had previously enjoyed their...catwatching.

The songsters, wren and robin, stayed loyal and true all winter long.

The darkest morning was heralded and cheered by their sweetness and life.

And soon, more came in, for food in the neediest days, when frost padlocked the earth, and there was little to be had.

When the badgers made great scrapes in the earth digging for worms and slugs...

A pair of blue tits, oh so bright...

Chaffinches in their muted beauty.

Always a couple of robins, vying and fighting for crumbs.

Later, there would be goldfinches.

And, as spring neared, a large speckled thrush alighted atop the old stone wall near the door.

As if to introduce himself to Sister, before flying to the very top of the tallest tree to sing his heart out there.

But the prettiest and most engaging of all were the wagtails.

Black and white charmers, with their running dance, and the long, slender tail that wagged continuously like a child's wind-up toy.

They preferred the ground to any feeder, and Sister would hold her breath at their fearless audacity when the cats were near.

As spring came, Sister became aware that the pair of these who had adopted the bird table were coming in more often than any other birds.

To and fro, to and fro.

All day long.

Always there was one flying in.

When the table was empty, they came to the window and called to her.

"Please feed us!"

Sister was intrigued.

And she set up a feeding tray on the wide window ledge, just for them.

Soon, their vigil became frenzied.

Sister watched them; they were clearly nesting and had young to feed.

They flew two fields away, and were
busy all day long, leaving the window
with beaks full of food.

Calling keenly if the tray was empty.

Week after week their faithful flights
lasted.

Then it eased off a little, so Sister
assumed that the babies had flown.

Until the next morning when she was
sitting outside the door in warm sun,
knitting.

And suddenly there were it seemed
wagtails everywhere.

The two she knew, and younger ones
with paler plumage.

Seven in all!

Perfect small birds, their tails
wagging coquettishly in their inimitable
fashion.

The birds had brought their family to show Sister, before chasing them off to start their own life.

She sat there, surrounded by running, dipping birds, almost in tears of delight.

Chapter Three

Her mind on feathered ones, Sister went
to pick leaves to add to her simple meal.

A grand mixture there was just now,
from growing plants.

Turnip tops, just a leaf or three from
each plant...a few tiny kale shoots...and
a little early purple broccoli, yielded a
serving.

This had been the way for all the years
she had grown.

Picking and gleaning...

And always plenty for larger feathered
ones to share.

And her first cockerel came to mind,
with his gentle ways.

A Rooster called Rooney...

It was Sister's first year on the island.

Autumn had been almost over when she came, with the long, dark Northern winter ahead of her.

Once she had found her feet and settled in, her thoughts, as she got to know her scattered neighbours, turned to all things growing and mutually nurturing.

The ancient symbiotic relationships that man has always relied on.

The old, old ways of as near self-sufficiency as was possible appealed to her monastic nature.

Planning and dreaming in dark winter evening, as she knitted by the glow of the peat fire, seeing bright images amid the flames.

The hermitage had a good patch of land around it; rough and overgrown, but wide.

And there was a byre and a shed also.

Hens did well there.

There were no natural predators, you see. No foxes or weasels.

And the great black-backed gulls would not tackle a full-grown bird.

So hens could be completely free range.

Many houses had them pecking around; old ways reminding of old days.

And to have fresh eggs...Still warm from the hen... With rich golden yolks...

Sometimes because of winter storms, supplies could be held up...

And the yolks of the battery ones from a neighbouring island were so pale.

As winter oh, so slowly yielded to spring, and the time came to think about the short summer, Sister asked around about acquiring some birds.

Soon, she was told, there would be point-of-lay pullets available, from the mainland.

Soon...

So she called the number she had been given, and, with great aplomb, ordered six!

And stocked up with bruised barley...
and bought a bale of hay for bedding...
and made some of the tea chests from
her move into neat nest-boxes.

It all felt very... professional indeed.

"There!" she said, dusting her hands off.
"All ready now! Snug as can be. All we
need now are the hens."

And, in due course, she had a 'phone call
telling her that her hens would be on the
evening boat.

As indeed they were.

She watched to see the boat creaming in
between the islands, and drove then
swiftly down to the pier, to be there
when her new little ones arrived.

The man who unloaded swung the crate
easily into the back of the car.

Sister tried not to look too eager as, after all, they were "only chickens."

Smiling all the short way at the agitated croonings and cluckings from behind her.

Speaking soft, soothing words to them, now that there was no-one to hear her and think her daft.

Once home, she eagerly opened the hatchback.

The crate was too heavy for her to move safely, so she started the car again, and drove carefully round the house.

And backed right up to the byre door.

It was almost dark.

Sister had read many stories carefully on the internet and asked around.

So she knew that once a hen had slept and roosted somewhere, there they would settle.

Like most birds, they "died" when darkness hovered.

So she opened the crate lid, and one by one gently lifted the birds out.

Oh, so soft and warm they were in her hands. Smooth, sleek, feathers... And quiet when held securely round the wings.

And, sure enough - and was it not wondrous when critters did as the books said - they each sought the top of the stall, ready to sleep.

Sister spoke gently to them, and decided to leave the car there for the night rather than risk panicking them by starting the engine again.

Just as she was about to go back to the house, something caught her eye in the crate. And there it was...

A tiny brown egg...

She laughed aloud.

Clearly the stress of the journey had brought this about - but it boded well for the future - and made a welcome treat for her.

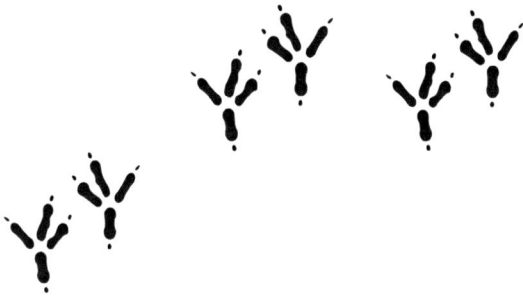

The hens kept her busy the next while.

They were "up" at dawn, pecking querulously around their new home, totally unused to grass and mud after the hatchery.

And they were tame and friendly;
dependent on her and following her
round whenever she appeared.

Running and flapping to her, wings
outspread, in the most engaging
manner.

The barley helped of course... Sister
loved to feed them from her hand, their
heads on one side, hard, eager beaks on
her skin.

Sharp, beady eyes.

Each different, in feathers, in shape, and
above all in character.

And a natural leader among them.

Sister had never realized these things.

So now she enjoyed the acquaintance
hugely.

As she did the eggs when they started in abundance.

The whole island was awash with eggs in the summer.

At every social event, egg sandwiches featured heavily.

And such eggs! Large, golden yolks.

One visitor thought Sister had put saffron in the sponge cake she served with afternoon tea, so yellow was it.

After a few weeks, a new thing occurred.

The hens, running in front of her, would, as soon as her shadow fell on them, stop suddenly and crouch, heart- shaped.

It became quite dangerous!

And the thought of wee fluffy chickens appealed more to Sister than she would admit.

So it was a cockerel that was needed now.

And no one on the island, at this season, had a spare one she could buy or beg.

But the Post Mistress had a relative on the mainland who had one she could let Sister have, if she would collect it.

So the next day, armed with precise instructions, off Sister went on the morning boat, the wee car driven carefully into the belly of the valiant little ferry boat that plied between the islands.

It was a fine day, and Sister sat on the top deck, revelling in the sun on her skin and the sea wind fresh on her skin.

The voyage, of well over an hour, fascinated.

The boat wound in and out of islands, and as often, there was someone nearby to tell her the names and a little more about them.

And she enjoyed a hot coffee from the canteen...

Such luxury; to sit and drink coffee atop a boat in the sun.

Life was rich indeed.

All too soon they were at the large island they called the mainland.

And Sister set about her shopping first.

There were several hours to fill before the boat back so the cockerel would be her last call.

The days out were a pleasure if the weather favoured them.

So Sister had an enjoyable day, and, all her errands done, and her picnic lunch - egg sandwiches of course - eaten at a quiet beach, headed for the farm.

The Post Mistress had told her that the niece was very big.

Sister had thought that this meant ... wide... and so she was somewhat surprised when the tallest person she had ever met appeared at the door.

Sister was not short, but this girl topped her by many inches.

The cockerel was ready; all packed in a box that had held a TV set.

Quiet and still as they loaded him into the back of the car, behind the boxes of groceries.

And he stayed quiet all the long voyage home.

Never a murmur or a movement from him.

Sister became quite concerned.

Off the ferry she drove and back up the narrow road to the hermitage.

Again, it was nearing darkfall, so again she unloaded the car quietly and released the bird in near-dark.

So it was not until the following morning that she was able to inspect her new charge.

She heard him as she was in early prayers, starting to crow... and smiled.

Clearly, there was nothing at all wrong with him.

And oh, he was a handsome fellow!

Rich brown in all tones and shades. A magnificent bird, with a long, curving tail of iridescent feathers.

A huge comb - with some strange black patches thereon.

(The Postmistress later confessed that they were bruises; that the old cockerel had attacked Rooney and would have killed him had Sister not asked for him. They had rinsed him off by dunking him in the cattle trough. Another life saved.)

As he swaggered around the yard, head held high and beak wide open in his proclamation.

I AM HERE!

I AM KING!

LOOK AT ME!

The girls were duly impressed, and later
that year - and this is of course a story
for another day - his first chicks were
hatched.

Why was he called Rooney? Oh, that too
is another tale...

Even before that, many farmers asked
for eggs from Sister, as he was new
blood to the island and thus his
offspring were in great demand.

And as the years passed, many chicks
were hatched and many grew up to lay
in their turn, in the rich cycle and
pattern of life.

And Rooney grew and waxed strong.

Until one day, many years later, Sister
went out to find him lying on the grass,
still alive but unable to walk.

She of course picked him up and took him inside to be cared for.

He had, it seemed, had a stroke, and although he recovered, Sister realized that if she were to go on breeding chicks, she would need another cockerel.

Because clearly Rooney would not last another season.

Her new boy came from a neighbouring island early in the year.

An exotic blue feathered creature, who followed her everywhere.

Until his adolescence passed.

The first inkling Sister had of the new state of affairs was when she saw Blue Boy attacking Rooney ferociously.

Hard at it they were, no holds barred.

A dreadful sight.

Sister threw a bucket of water over them; and it made not an iota of difference.

On they fought, neck ruffs up, spurs out.

Intent on murder.

Finally, she grabbed Rooney and dragged him away.

The land was large enough for the two, as they learned to keep to their territory.

Sister kept a close eye on them, smiling as the hens, numerous by then, split into two factions.

Each cockerel had his own harem.

But one day, she saw Rooney fall down again.

He crawled under the shed, but Blue Boy was quick to see his rival in trouble and swooped in, clearly bent on the kill this time.

Sister fought him off, and awkwardly extracted Rooney from his refuge.

Once more bleeding from his comb.

Blue Boy danced and crowed exultantly in victory as Rooney was carried off into the house, more dead than alive.

But he had crowed too soon, and reckoned without Sister's kind heart - and her love for and gratitude to a cockerel who had served faithfully for so many years.

The garden was fenced of course.

Else there would have been no garden.
Hens are mighty diggers.

So Sister took one of the crates from the byre, and set it well away from the fence, closely screened by rose hedging.

She filled it with fresh hay, and, with wire netting, made a small run alongside.

She washed the blood tenderly off Rooney's dazed head, and set him in his new home, with a dish of bread soaked in good goat milk - and of course, Blossom the goat is another story altogether.

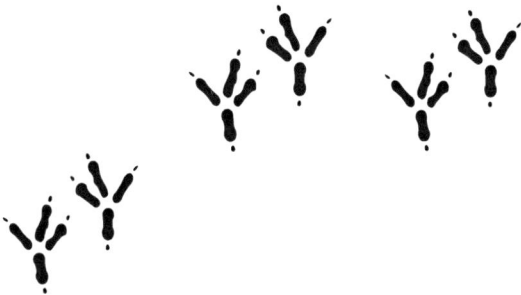

And so began the Indian summer of an old rooster called Rooney.

He pottered around part of the garden by day, and at night slept safe and snug in his wee retirement apartment.

Nothing worried him - except when Blue Boy, suspicious cockerel that he was, arrogant and proud, peered over the fence.

Then terror would fill Rooney's old eyes.

But danger soon passed, and the old one was at peace and happy.

And very companionable in his old age, as Sister sat by the door shelling peas, or knitting.

He would sit by her, crooning happily..

As he grew older, she would feed him from a spoon.

After all, she would be old one day too.

He slept more and more of course. And more and more deeply.

And one day, Sister found him lying on his side, claws curved, lifeless.

Her eyes misted over.

But he had had a rich and wonderful life.

So she went to fetch the spade.

For all her critters were buried nearby.

When she went back out, she was mystified.

Where was he?

Surely she had left him here, by the rose bush?

She searched around a while, frantic.

When something touched her ankle, she leapt sky high.

There he was; Rooney.

On his feet from the deepest of sleeps.

Head cocked, eyes bright.

As if to say, oh you cannot get rid of me that easily.

Cannot you tell sleep from death?

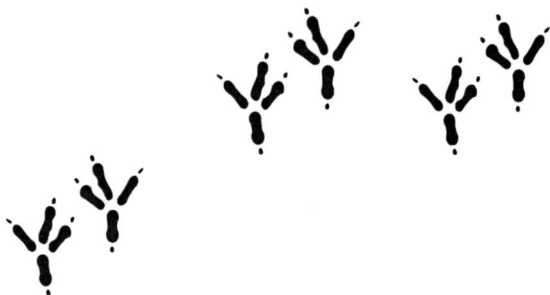

Sister chuckled.

And, remembering now through the tunnel of the years, she found she could hardly remember his real death.

More the life he lived all the years he was with her.

Chapter Four

The day continued fine and dry, and, after Noon Prayer and lunch, Sister migrated to the shore.

She had left an old deck chair down there now.

So she just had her work and refreshments to carry down the winding path, past the little white gate, and down the rocky trail to the sheltered cove.

Of course, she had followers...

Behind her, trailed Caro and Amanda, strolling insouciant.

Picking their way, dainty-pawed, through the grass.

Caro now fluffy and dry. And looking so spruce and lovely that Sister wondered if maybe a bath might become a regular event?

Maybe not, she smiled.

Their following reminded Sister of days long gone when there would have been two lambs, three cats and a lame hen in a straggling but determined line behind her.

Ah, tales for different times!

The shore was never the same on any two days.

Always new shells and pebbles; always sky and sea changing.

So first a slow wander along the tide line, bag in hand, collecting interesting bits.

Shells and pretty pebbles... Interesting scraps of driftwood...

Always new folk too...

Today, a pair of wild ducks was fossicking around in the banks of sea weed.

Nesting time was near.

Such delightful creatures, wild and shy, but safe here.

And as Sister settled to work, the cats at her feet, other ducks came to her mind.

Dilly, Dolly and Dally,
the Hermitage Ducks ...

It was Annabel who started it.

The idea of ducks.

Not that Sister needed much encouragement where all things furred and feathered featured.

Since coming to the island, her fascination with all that contributed to self-sufficiency, be it for the food they gave, or simply their beauty - or, as she saw loveliness in them all - both, had grown and grown.

As a visiting minister put it, she soon had a menagerie.

Although Sister was not pleased at that name.

For these were workers, these critters of hers.

Annabel was English, and heavily into serious New Age things…strictly vegetarian, a lover of animals, in ways that made the islanders chuckle or scorn her.

When the farmer who had given her an orphan lamb told her off when he saw her giving the year old ram a bottle of milk, Annabel tossed her tangled mane of henna'd hair in complete impenitence.

"He enjoys it," she declared. "And he is mine."

So Sister found a ready ally in her acquisition of ever yet more creatures.

And in her love of them for their own sweet sakes.

Not ever to be...eaten.

Annabel had ducks.

Sister had no idea where she had obtained them from, but was sure they had been saved from orange sauce in their coming to her.

And that year, three of the ducks had taken it into their pretty white heads to lay and nest at a distance from the small house where Annabel lived.

Although there were no foxes or other four-legged predators, the black-backed gulls were a constant threat, to eggs and young alike, so Annabel worried and fretted over the safety of the small colony.

And, of course, Sister worried alongside her when she called at the hermitage.

And they pondered together on ducks.

The island was criss-crossed with drainage ditches, and in places, hers had worn the banks away so that there was a natural small lagoon...

Ah, ducks would love that.

And the eggs, while too oily for her taste, were excellent for the baking Sister loved to do.

Rich fruit cakes especially benefited greatly from duck eggs.

Of course, as both Sister and Annabel knew, that was simply a rationalization and a justification.

For the love of ducks.

Although Annabel also loved Sister's fruit cakes - as did her two teenaged children.

When the duck eggs hatched, there were no less than twenty seven, the vast majority of them female.

So Annabel's next task was to find new homes where they would not be... eaten.

That would be a condition of sale or gift.

Non - negotiable.

And woe betide anyone later found to have defaulted on that promise.

And of course, Sister was almost first on Annabel's list of safe, reliable adopters for her ducklings.

So the price of a fruit cake per duck was settled on.

And in due course, Annabel arrived, breathless and hair flying - for, you understand, ducks can run pretty fast when they are being pursued by a lady and two teenagers - with a big sack..

And they released the three pretty white ducks at the back of the hermitage.

What a commotion from the hens and cockerels... squawks and flapping and crowing...

Small wonder the ducks, in a neat line, headed for the wilder part of the wild land surrounding the hermitage, tails waddling frantically in their haste.

Sister and Annabel watched anxiously, then shrugged and went inside, trusting that the newcomers would settle in at their own pace.

And peace descended with the coming of night, soft and silent.

The following morning, Sister eagerly emerged at first light, to greet her new family.

She searched every ditch and clump of rushes, the hens following her in a worried crowd, crooning querulously.

Not a duck to be seen.

It was too early to 'phone Annabel, or to go round to see her.

So Sister watched and waited, fed the hens and cats, and tried to settle to her work.

Every few minutes she would check outside again for her missing charges.

When the 'phone rang, she knew it would be Annabel, and sure enough it was.

All twenty seven of the young ducks, that she had so laboriously chased and caught and driven to various farms and houses all over the island, had returned to her.

Homing ducks...

Sister's hermitage was a good half mile away, and the mental image of three white ducks waddling determinedly down the middle of the road in pitch dark was ...

Many months later, Sister realized that that should have prepared her for what ducks were really like...

Feisty, willful, and characters to be reckoned with.

But at the time, she did not think.

They were simply pretty birds with smiling beaks.

Who laid, in spring, beautiful rich eggs.

Many had walked miles to return home.

From all parts of the island.

An innate mysterious homing instinct that had Sister marveling - even while she commiserated, biting her cheek to stop the laughter, with Annabel.

One incomer was insisting that Annabel bring her back the same ducklings as she had named them all already.

They laid their plans very carefully the next time.

And when the car arrived with the large, wriggling sack, Sister had ready the coop she used for new chicks, in full view of the back windows.

Oh, so carefully, they extracted one indignant young duck at a time, and incarcerated them in the wide meshed coop, where food and water were ready.

Even a large bowl to bathe in...

Three noisy rebels, and a brouhaha in the farmyard...

It is amazing the decibels an outraged duck can manage.

So they left them to it, having timed the arrival for soon before dark.

They reckoned, having consulted more experienced duck keepers than they were - and seen a few badly concealed smirks in the process - that a week would see the ducks settled.

So each day, Sister gave them a large bowl of water to bathe in, and abundant food.

And paid no heed to their pleadings.

It was then that she realized that she would never be able to tell them apart.

They were pure white with no tones or differences.

Identical in every way.

So she simply called them by a generic triplet of Dilly, Dolly, and Dally.

Liberation day came.

Sister knew it was no use waiting until dark as they were clearly partly nocturnal from their previous escapade.

Still, she decided to wait until dark as then there would be less traffic on the road, should they again decide to go home.

And, with breath suspended and a prayer on her lips, she opened the large door of the coop and said, "OK, ladies. Freedom..."

Not a one moved, so Sister shrugged and left them to it.

Realizing by now that there was more to ducks than met the eye.

And when morning came, she looked out hesitantly - to see the trio in the ditch, splashing with great glee.

Upending in that engaging duck way.

And a great sigh of relief escaped her.

Clearly they had decided to stay.

They were young of course, so would live
the winter out in peace.

Unless you kept ducks in a lighted shed,
they only lay in spring.

They were very different from hens,
Sister found.

Much more soncy and independent.

Not the tame little feather-headed birds
the hens were.

They would never eat from her hand.

Yet their charm was irresistible.

Their noisy, clumsy race across the yard
when she emerged to feed the flock
never ceased to make Sister smile.

And in the dark, wet winter, smiles were
always welcome.

There was something so captivating
about their beaming beaks.

And the zest and joy with which they upended in the pool.

And their guzzling eating habits.

Slurping in the mud with no inhibitions or manners.

Not forgetting Sir Francis...

In the early months of the year, Sister started the search for a drake.

By now she was skilled in the care of tiny chicks, and the thought of ducklings was even more irresistible than that of chicks.

And one was promised from a neighbouring farm at a reasonable price.

Sister was expecting a plain white fellow.

And thus planning a simple name.

But when the sack was opened and this glorious bird emerged - to be cooped of course - words failed.

All colours and hues of green and blue he was.

So what else would do but Sir Francis...

A regal name for an aristocratic bird.

The girls loved him and made a great fuss of him - which is when Sister began to realize what social creatures ducks are.

And when the time came, they started laying.

They chose a large clump of reeds across the land at the back that year.

Well away from the house of course, yet easily visible.

Sister watched, intrigued, as she "stole" a few eggs the first few days.

When they were out feeding of course.

That is when she learned what the quack they made that sounded like maniacal laughter meant.

Dilly - or Dolly or Dally - crept up behind her and scared her half to death with a loud, raucous cackle.

Staring at her accusingly.

And across the field came the cavalry.

Dilly and Dolly - or whichever combination it was - with Sir Francis leading the way.

Sister hastily hid the eggs up the wide sleeve of her habit, and pleaded complete innocence as she faced the circle of loudly quacking birds.

It was unnerving!

But the eggs were plentiful - as long as she harvested them swiftly before the guard duck raised the alarm.

For they were highly organized indeed.

When they settled to sit, she realized that they were in fact all three sharing the nest.

In and out of the rushes they would come and go.

Sometimes one, sometimes two.

Sister asked Annabel, who assured her that this was normal, but that it meant sometimes that they did not sit properly and that hatchings were thus poor.

The days and weeks passed; patient ducks and patient Sister.

Longing to see the ducks emerge with a line of fluffy yellow ducklings behind them.

But all was not to be safe and simple that year.

There was almost always a terrible storm in those waters at the end of May or early in June.

And that year was the worst for many years.

It struck the day the ducklings were due to hatch.

And Sister struggled in the gale and rain across to the nest.

To find mayhem.

In their terror, the ducks had sat too tightly, and had squashed several partly-hatched babies to death.

Tears added to the rain streaming down Sister's chilled face.

She resolutely then took in all the as yet unhatched eggs, so try to prevent yet more fatalities.

The outcry from the ducks was of course appalling.

Pathetic, heartbroken quacks from already distressed birds.

And Sister had to turn her face away as they buffeted her.

She groped under the birds for the eggs.

Soft, indignant, duck-down breasts.

Then she fought the gale all the way back across the field, with the quacking echoing in her ears.

Soaked through, swiftly she changed, and set up the improvised incubator that she used at such times.

And the long night began.

At the end of it, there were just two ducklings.

Sister was not alone in the losses that day.

Many had been hard hit.

So they all had a great deal of sympathy for each other, which was comforting indeed.

And oh! The wonder of the tiny birds. The miniature beaks, and that waterproof down.

And those tiny webbed feet.

When the weather calmed, she brought the little ones to the coop, and managed to herd the ducks in with them while she made a bigger pen.

Or, rather, after netting the beds, gave them the use of part of the garden.

For flat-footed ducks make a terrible mess of growing things.

To pen them was very necessary that year.

So many wild bird fledglings had been destroyed, swept off the cliff nurseries by the great storm, that predators, the great black-backed gulls among them, were getting bold and desperate in their search for food for their own young.

Anything small was easy meat; and they were even taking cat food from outside back doors.

And a duckling would make a wonderful meal for them.

So the ducklings needed to be near the house for their own safety.

The ducks however, did not appreciate Sister's intervention.

They treated her like a kidnapper.

After all, she had form, as she had stolen their babies once already.

She was to be carefully watched.

And at every stage, they managed to escape with their precious babies, from the safe confines of the garden.

Sister lost count of the number of times she cornered the ducklings and carried them back to the safety of the garden, Dilly, Dolly and Dally in noisy pursuit.

They crossed the ditched to the neighbouring fields, in among the tall hay and barley...

Meanwhile, Sir Francis, his work for the year done, was having his own wee dramas.

Ducks are sociable birds.

And the drake from the farm across the back fields, decided to come and stay a while.

Maybe the food was better? Or just time for the men to get together?

Sir Francis was fine for a few days.

They pottered about together quite companionably.

Then he seemed to adopt the maxim that guests, like fish, stink after three days.

And the fights began.

Drake fights are amazing things; they buffet and bluff.

So Sister called her neighbour to please collect his drake before they battered each other to death.

It took them an hour to corner and catch the wily bird.

Finally the farmer chased him out of the byre, while Sister stood at the door, habit spread out.

Goal!

And off went the farmer carrying the intruder.

And peace descended once more as the year started to wane.

And the young were grown and out of danger.

Fine young ducks, with bright, intelligent eyes.

Peace then in a short autumn day, splashing in the full ditches together.

Days to rest and prepare for winter.

The following year, the ducks decided to avoid the rushes where they had fared so badly the previous year.

Wise birds.

They chose first to lay under the large shed.

So Sister had to take a broom handle to extricate the eggs.

Once more attracting the loud quacking and accusing circle of ducks.

As she told, them, they could not sit under there; there was no real shelter after all.

They agreed with her on that.

As the next day she found they had laid in Blossom's stall.

And would not be moved.

So Blossom was now milked alongside her stall, under protest of course.

It was then that Sister saw the full extent of duck-society.

The first time, she could scarcely believe it.

As she was milking the goat, with one white duck enthroned on her splendid nest, along came the other four ducks, led by Sir Francis.

They surrounded the nest, crooning quietly, and tweaked at the straw, tidying the nest and tucking her in safely and cosily.

For all the world like visitors to a hospital...

And every night this was the ritual.

Sister smiled now at these memories, watching the wild ducks play and forage.

Waddling on their great, flat feet, or swimming fast and gracefully, playing at the water's edge, where all manner of interesting bits were creamed in at the racing tide.

She would see them often now, she suspected.

And their babies, when that time came.

And this time, there would be a line of fluffy ducklings, swimming joyfully after their parents.

All would be well...

Chapter Five

Early, very early, the following day,
Sister set off for the nearest large town.

This was her way on summer days; to do
the bulk of her shopping before the
world was up.

For a big shop there was open all day
and night.

The roads were quiet and empty; the air
pure and clear.

So off she drove, the car empty.

The route she preferred was a little
longer, but was through open, wild land,
forested, lakes shining, wild flowers and
birds in abundance.

She carried a small picnic stove now,
and would stop partway, and have a
quiet breakfast.

This she was enjoying when she saw, wondrous sight, a herd of wild goats on the land by the roadside.

All colours and sizes, and with a large, fearsomely horned Billy Goat Gruff clearly in charge.

Tiny kids tagging along with their mothers... half grown weanlings.

Piebald, black, white – and oh look! A brown one... Just like Blossom...

A Goat called Blossom.

On the island, many goats lived.

It was interesting that all of these belonged to incomers.

Who had moved to the island with thoughts and plans of self-sufficiency.

It was a pattern. Hens, a goat, maybe a few sheep...

Grow vegetables.

The dream of the city folk.

So it was only natural that Sister started to think seriously about a goat of her own.

There was land enough around the cottage that was her hermitage, and a good barn to house her at night.

The hens roosted in the rafters, but there was plenty of room.

Sister of course by now had her own eggs, in rich abundance, and the garden was starting to yield all the vegetables she could need.

It was thus logical enough to seek a source of fresh milk in this increasingly self-sufficient life of hers.

For that was a part of the charm and industry of this life apart.

In this island setting especially, and in the Holy Poverty she was Vowed to.

So she began to ask around, and to read up what keeping a nanny goat involved.

The library sent the books she requested in her next Library Box - for this was how books came to the island in those days.

Encased in stout leather boxes according to the reader's wishes and likes.

After reading all she could, she began to look around at the island stock.

Her first actual research was at the small farm nearest to her.

Where two white goats grazed.

They were close-tethered, staked out each day for fresh grass.

The owner, an incomer like herself, was at times a rather difficult person, impatient and never seeing that others could do the things she did well.

Or maybe she thought that Nuns were weak and helpless creatures.

As if!

For Sister was the only Nun the island had ever known.

And all kinds of strange ideas emerged from time to time.

Which she counteracted in her own ways as the years wore on.

Winning in turn respect for the fine baking that found its way quietly to many a home where there was sickness or grief.

Seeing the postman out in the bad weather with a skimpy old hat, she had knitted him a fine new one in navy with a smart red trim, simply leaving it where he put the letters.

And each Christmas she made him an apple pie, suitably decorated.

The Post Mistress told her much later that he had been so excited by this.

"She made me an apple pie with stars on it..."

Small ways to care.

But this lady was harder to approach.

She had moved there as a widow with a small child, and had had a hard life farming for herself in what was still a man's world.

Winning at last great respect.

But, if somewhat offhand and unwelcoming, she allowed - rather than invited - Sister to call round at milking time one afternoon.

Sister had the distinct and lasting impression that the owner was determined to put her off keeping a goat.

When she untethered her two, she set off across the road and to the byre at a spanking rate, not waiting to see if Sister could keep up.

Sister of course could, and thus arrived in the barn, keeping discreetly back, to see the first goat being tethered fore and aft; immobilized in fact.

The white milk spurted speedily - and Sister knew by now that goat's milk was very white - and the goat kept reaching backwards to drink it...

A sideways glance from the lady had Sister keeping her expression ... interested.

Nuns know a lot more about human nature and foibles than most folk realize.

So she was very careful to mask her feelings.

After the eccentric goats had been milked, the lady vanished into the house without a word, and Sister wended her way home, thoughtful indeed.

No way would she treat an animal like that...

Or, and she smiled as she closed the gate carefully behind her, allow it to waste its milk like that.

So she sought a goat further afield.

Which led her to old Tom Goatbeard.

Another incomer he was, living right at the far end of the island.

He had the only billy goat on the island - as was very, very obvious if you were near him.

Sister once was behind him in the tiny wooden Post Office.

She wondered at first what the indescribable stench was and where it was coming from - until the Post Mistress winked at her.

And as soon as old Tom had left, she whipped out an air freshener spray and used it liberally...

Which, Sister thought, was really as bad as the stink of billy goat.

If that were possible.

It was as bad a smell as they come.

Indescribably horrible and never forgotten.

And the man reeked of it.

But yes, old Tom had a nanny he could let her have.

Not a baby, and in milk already.

She had given birth to triplets in fact.

So off Sister went to the mainland on the boat to equip herself with all that the book on goats the Library had supplied in her Library Box advised.

And to the huge emporium that sold every type of paint, hardware, garden equipment, farming supplies... the range made the head reel.

She was seeking a collar, a chain, and a swivel.

For the goat, whatever she later decided, would need to be tethered a while especially while she was being milked.

The swivel?

Was to stop her twisting the rope or chain and... throttling herself.

The latter had the young man assistant foxed.

And Sister felt very knowledgeable and expert when she explained what it was for.

And he yelled to a mate… " WAL-TER! Need a swivel… for a GO … AT!"

Everyone turned and stared…

But the right tack was found… and Sister put the items in a rather pretty blue bucket… for the milk she would so soon have.

And bought a sack of flaked maize as well as goat mix.

She was enjoying this hugely of course.

And the next day, along came old Tom Goatbeard with his wee trailer, on which the new resident at the Hermitage stood enthroned.

For all the world like a royal personage on a street tour among her subjects.

She allowed Tom to lead her down the ramp, then stared at Sister with a look of such utter disdain.

Such as Sister had not known since her very early days as a Novice.

It was quite unnerving.

The goat was dark brown. She had horns, toggles, those strange appurtenances, and a dainty wee curling beard.

And her oblong- pupilled oblique eyes were hostile and unblinking.

Tom showed her how easy she was to milk.

And, sure enough, for him the milk flowed easily.

Sister wisely decided then to keep her calm, and her reputation intact, so assured old Tom she would be fine.

That they needed time to get to know each other, and for the goat to settle in.

Old Tom looked a little... disappointed, but led the goat to the newly made stall - constructed of course of old wooden pallets - and closed the door - also made of an old wooden pallet.

Sister paid him, then purposefully stood by the open gate.

So that all Old Tom Goatbeard could do was drive out.

Leaving Sister to face her new and clearly hostile critter.

She wisely left the goat to herself for a wee while, as the hens, who had scattered, came clucking and crooning querulously back.

And half an hour later, after a restoring cup of coffee, she resolutely picked up the bucket, filled the plastic food bowl with the sweet smelling goat mix, and sallied forth to this new challenge.

The goat eyed her beadily as she opened the door of the stall.

Then her face was buried in the food...

When Sister crouched to put the bucket under her, she lay down on it.

Just as the library book said she would !

Amazing!

Sister pondered for just a moment.

Then she removed the food bowl from the goat's munching face.

Trying not to worry about those sharp, curved horns.

The goat turned her head, outraged.

Sister held the bowl out again - just too far for the goat to reach unless she stood up again.

The goat rose, and moved forward.

And under went the bucket again.

And Sister managed to squeeze the full teats once - before the heavy, hairy body once more sank atop the pretty blue bucket.

Sister chatted the while; about how intimate a work it was after all.

And the dance went on.

Food moved, goat up, milk squeezed out, goat down, food moved...

Sister was not going to be beaten.

And after half an hour, she had managed to extract a cupful of white milk.

So she made do with that, and left the goat to ruminate on the matter.

The milk was sweet and untainted.

Unlike some goat milk.

And the next morning, Sister was there again.

And by the time another half hour had elapsed, the goat was happier and a little more accommodating.

As long as there was her favourite food before her.

And Sister was growing more skilled at the milking, learning how to squeeze, how to mimic a kid by thumping the udder gently.

For the book had stressed that she must empty the udder each time or the milk supply would of course reduce as demand eased.

Weary and hot, but feeling extremely pleased with herself, Sister lead her new charge out and across the field to tether her to graze.

It felt so good to be doing that.

And the goat settled in her smart new collar, butting at any hen that came anywhere near her.

Sister made a milk pudding that day - and an egg custard.

Life was good, very good indeed...

And as the weeks wore on that summer, the milk flowed and the eggs abounded and the garden produced all manner of good things.

And Sister ate well and richly.

Beautiful egg custards, milk puddings of all kinds, yoghurt...

Quiches, with home-grown vegetables...

She started also making cheese.

A soft curd cheese that was delicious, and also, with an improvised but effective press, hard cheese that would take some weeks to mature.

There was no end of the ideas and recipes.

After a while, Sister tried letting Blossom, for she had abandoned the rather outlandish name Old Tom had given the goat, run free.

To discover that she was a skilled escape artist who loved to socialize with any sheep that were around.

Watching Blossom rounding up and chasing a flock of sheep over the road, she wondered if goats could be shot for sheep worrying.

But no one said anything - well, not to her face at least.

And there was nothing she could do unless that were so.

There were two major offences that led to Blosson being re- tethered.

One was her ability to leap the fence into the hard-won garden.

Goats will eat almost anything with great relish.

And all Sister's work on mending the fence was to no avail when the crafty goat was concerned.

Through the wire the horns would go, and where the horns went, the rest would soon follow...

Or if she got hopelessly stuck, there she would stay until Sister realized, and went to release her.

The second offence?

Sister had a hysterical phone call from the Chairwoman of the Community Council...

Blossom had twice hidden in the ditch and leaped out just as she was driving past.

The first time had been tolerated, but twice was too much.

This was, the island population being so small that folk tended to wear two or more hats, her friend at the Post Office.

Who Sister would not have offended for
the world.

So back went the collar and toggle and
chain - for a rope would be easily
chewed through.

And the lugubrious long face of the goat
would reproach Sister...

Until she was out of sight when Blossom
would cheer up and start enjoying the
grass once more.

She was a supreme tragedy queen.

So affectionate also.

In the long summer evenings, she would
roam free for an hour or so, under close
supervision, chasing the chickens and
kicking up her heels in sheer joy.

Then she would come to Sister, to nuzzle
and butt her, and eat treats from her
hand. Bits of brown bread, carrot tops,
apple cores.

All would be thoughtfully chewed in rapt concentration.

Once, someone had given Sister a bag of boiled fruit sweets, which she was not keen on.

And she could not resist offering Blossom one.

Oh, what a treat!

The goat rolled it round in her mouth, deep in thoughtful appreciation, sucking with such huge pleasure.

And on fine days, when Sister went a-walking, she would take Blossom with her.

Along the grassy track to the shore where the seals played.

There she would be tethered safely to a post while Sister sat and knitted.

And, her fill eaten, the goat would cuddle onto Sister's habit, to chew the cud noisily and soulfully.

Following her then home for all the world like a great dog.

A thousand memories and images came to Sister's happy mind.

The spring day when the daffodils, long awaited after the long, severe northern winter had started to unfurl their pure gold of joy...

Sister glanced out of the window and saw to her horror that Blossom had somehow got loose...

She gave chase immediately stubbing her toe agonizingly on the stone doorstep - to see Blossom sail back elegantly over the fence.

Legs tucked in like a showjumper, with a daffodil dangling rakishly from her mouth.

Blossom sulking when the geese arrived, jealous of the newcomers, staring reproachfully at Sister and refusing to let her milk down for two worrying days.

Blossom wandering thigh deep in the tall, rippling field buttercups that abounded, gazing out to sea, eyes narrowed against the breeze.

As that first autumn neared - and in that northern clime autumn is early and sudden - Sister asked around other goat owners on neighbouring islands.

Milk is seasonal. It is intended to feed the young of the species, who of course by winter are fully grown.

So then it tails off and there is none until the next spring's new birth.

Sister pondered long on this. She knew by now that the only billy goat on the island was Blossom's sire.

More, she knew too that kids were killed at birth more often than not; hence the sire mattered not.

So, quietly, she made her decision, after much thought and prayer, to try to keep Blossom in milk through the winter.

As others did and do.

If she failed, she would think again.

As autumn ripened and fled, and Blossom came in and out of season, the milk dwindled.

It was richer than ever, but far less of it.

And wondrously, Blossom and Sister came through the long winter in fine form.

With great patience and perseverance.

And the milk grew in abundance again; never as much as that first year, but sufficient for Sister's needs.

And that was so for all the years they were together; Sister and her redoubtable nanny goat, Blossom.

It was only when she was about to leave the island that she finally heard that this was being talked about with great awe.

A goat still in milk for all those years without bearing a kid.

And she realized that had she not been who she was, or in an earlier time, she would have been thought of as being a witch.

As it was, there was the power of Prayer to think of...

Of the lovingkindness and caring for all critters that Prayer enfolds.

That can achieve more than most would ever know.

A truth that Sister and all her Sisters knew and rested in with every breath they took.

Chapter Six

It clouded as Sister was about her shopping, and by the time she was ready to come home, the soft Irish rain was sweeping across the landscape.

Dove grey skies; shrouded forests.

Lambs in the fields clinging near their mothers in the wetness.

She meandered gently homewards, her thought drawn irresistibly to other lambs, smaller than these fat ones.

One especially.

The Thursday Lamb...

That year, it rained all Holy Week.

That "soft" Irish rain, that soaks all it touches, silent downpour, hushed and grey-veiled.

Sweeping, visible water, across the land.

It was of course a week for Prayer and Silence.

But after the Wednesday, Sister needed to be out of the hermitage a while.

Before the Triduum and Easter Day.

To walk quietly where the soft wind whispered.

So in the early afternoon, she donned her oldest habit in deference to the weather- something she would later be deeply grateful for - and over all her voluminous rain cape.

And on went her sturdy Wellingtons...

And the cats were left, peaceably asleep by the banked- up fire.

Sister needed to stretch her legs, and to be away from the environs a while.

To explore a little more the land over the bridge that was the entrance to the hermitage.

So up the winding drive she strode.

Filling her lungs with the moist, clean air.

Lifting her face to the drenching rain that soon dripped down her cheeks.

Across the bridge she paused.

Watching the grey swathes of water sheering across the pewter sea.

Visible weather...

Where cloud ended and rain began it was impossible to see.

Cloudfall; mist drop.

She had driven this way, but not yet walked it.

So now she set off briskly down the narrow lane, to see what she could see.

Past a ruined house.

So she stopped to explore that.

Little more than the gable end and chimney left - and from the chimney a tree was growing.

A rowan.

The doorway and window spaces were clear cut still, and the old hearth.

Niches in the stone surround were irresistible.

And her questing fingers were startled to find an old knife in a triangular hole.

Evocative of a life lived many years ago.

Carved out in a poor land.

So many of these old ruins; many built before the Great Famine.

Long, long deserted.

Poignant and sad.

On she walked, thoughtfully now, and
more slowly, as the waters of the
heavens surrounded her and dripped off
the bottom of the cape.

She passed many fields of sheep, always
pausing to watch the lambs.

They were a constant delight to her.

New life at this time.

Symbolic of the love of God in Jesus.

And even in the rain, they were playful
on the sodden ground.

Racing and leaping, then running full
tilt to butt the ewes in search of the rich,
fatty milk.

There was a Landrover parked near one
field.

The farmer was there, with another
man.

And they paused when they saw her, and started to come over to the gate.

Sister was still fairly new at that time - the object of much curiosity thus, as she seldom went out, and as her gate bore a large sign that brooked no casual entry.

So now she waited...

It was maybe time to meet these neighbours on their own ground.

The three chatted a while; Sister admiring the fine lambs, the farmer quizzing her, most unsuccessfully, on her life and origins.

For Nuns have no past. We are they who leave family and home for Jesus, simply. And there is no looking back then.

Something that sits uncomfortably with the Irish culture that is family and clan-based.

The rain grew heavier, and the farmer was about to set off for home, when Sister spied something amiss with a ewe at the other side of the field.

Remember, that she had lived many years on the island where sheep were the main source of income.

And although she had never been closely involved with lambing, she had learned a great deal.

And she knew thus that the main cause of death when lambs were a-birthing was what she could see now.

The lamb needs to come out with its two front legs ahead of it, you see.

Neatly tucked in under its throat.

So that when the next contraction comes, it does not literally strangle it.

And what she could see now was a tiny head out but no feet.

The farmer, his helper, and Sister, set off across the muddy field apace.

Leaping and running through rushes and mud.

And instinctively split up to surround the ewe.

Who was a wild one, in pain, and hard to catch thus.

They finally ran her down by the fence, in thick mud, among the rushes.

Which was when Sister, who sat on the ewe to immobilize her, was very, very glad she was wearing her oldest habit.

The farmer pulled the lamb out with force majeur and in great haste.

But it lay, steaming with birth fluid, on the muddy ground.

Lifeless, deflated.

So still and so flat, without the breath of life in it.

The farmer shrugged.

And made to stand up.

But Sister refused to let him give up.

"Shake it!" she ordered, praying in her heart as he did so.

To no avail.

Lord, she prayed. Not death; not on this Holy Day; not so near the life of Easter.

Please, Lord Jesus.

Lamb of God, life for this little lamb on this Holy Day.

Quite when the prayer became vocal, she never knew.

But then she was praying out loud, pleading for life for this new lamb, as the rain soaked them all, and the frail body grew chilled and seemed to shrink.

All on an Irish mountain field, in drenching rain.

And she saw it then as if from the sky; three tiny figures, helpless against death.

Lost in a field on a great mountain.

Insignificant, powerless, puny.

They were humouring her of course.

Thinking she could not face a dead lamb, that she would weep and embarrass them.

Thinking she knew nothing.

But, taught by stern Irish Sisters, they submitted to her authority automatically.

And the emotion of her imploring prayer moved them deeply.

"Please, please Lord Jesus; life for this lamb on Holy Thursday, Please, Lord; life for this tiny one on this Holy Time."

By then almost ten minutes had elapsed.

And the farmer was wondering how to extricate himself from this impossible situation without provoking a storm from Sister.

Suddenly, the lamb convulsed, as if an electric current had passed through it, and was still again.

And he stood up firmly. "That's it; it's gone."

And his mate nodded assent.

But Sister's smile lit up the sky.

"LOOK! He is breathing!"

And so he was, the big ram lamb...

Breathing well, his sides filling out as that precious life filled him.

And then he struggled to his shaky feet...

And the three stood back and let the ewe get up in her ungainly way.

And the farmer put the lamb to her, and they crept away.

And the farmer said, "That lamb was dead..."

There was nothing else he could say.

And as they drove away, Sister lingered to watch the lamb take his first milk.

"Lamb of God...We thank and bless you for this life, for this promise of life."

And she too went her way home in the gathering dusk.

Suddenly exhausted and chilled.

To soak in a hot bath and ponder the day.

Of life and Life; of lambs and of the Lamb of God.

Of the miracles of faith and prayer.

Postscript...

And so the year passes, and the years pass.

For Sister-on-the- mountain, and all her Sisters, wherever and however they live this life, the sweetness of hands busy, giving skills lent to them, and passing then that bright torch of loving and surrendering on.

Seasons and years...

Old Nun, in springtime sun..
Her music the birds' sweet orison...
Fingers flying through fine cream wool...
A shawl for a baby she will never see,
Far away across the sea...

Old Nun in summer rain,
Watching the streaming window pane,
Hands working a rainbow of mitts,
For winter- children she will never see,
Far away across the sea...

Old Nun in autumn gales,
Seeing the green world fade and pale,
Lap heaped high with thick warm hats,
For old and cold she will never meet,
Far away across the sea...

Old Nun in winter snow -
Homeward-bound.. not far to go.
Winding white wool ....slow, pensive
hands,
Rapt in the dove-wings heavenly
dance...
To be worked by Sisters she will never
see...
Far away across the sea...

Seasons of soul, seasons of heart,
Seasons together, seasons apart...
Rain and snow, wind and rain...
Mattering nothing, the ache or the
pain....

Always the Son, always that gain
Of love given freely, of life fully shared,
Of heaven on earth, of Jesus in heart.

Always the love, that bright,
strongwrought thread...
Enfolding, embracing, a healing of
heaven.

Many times are we asked, how we began, who was our Foundress, the where, the when... the why.

Many times there has been the intention to write all these things and more, but always there are other things.

For hungry children come before all else.

And when the Order almost died out a score or more years ago, all the records were left in a damp cellar in England.

They were, in that sad state, taken to Canada when the Mother House moved there, and when our Convent there was washed away by floods, once more they were saturated.

The task of trying to salvage is a time -consuming and heart breaking one.

For we cannot afford to get this done professionally.

But we have also many memories passed down orally...

And so now "The Legend of Mother Luke" is being written, and will be published later.

We offer here a summary of that inspiring and fascinating work.

The Legend of Mother Luke...

.... being the story of Sisters of Grace.

Once upon a time, there was a young girl who loved Jesus more than she loved her life, and longed to serve Him in the poor with all her heart and soul and mind and strength.

When she was only sixteen, she ran away from her rich home, for she was gently and nobly born, to earn her own living, so she could give all she earned to the very poor who thronged the streets.

For she knew that if she stayed where she was, soon she would be married off...

And the Spouse she sought was Jesus Christ.

Had she entered a convent, her contact with the poor would be strictly limited, and that was not what Jesus was asking of her.

She worked in a noisy, dirty factory by day and served the street people after the long hours there.

Soon they knew her goodness and kindness, that she was one of them and kept nothing back for herself.

As years went on, more women sought her out to live with her, and to do the work for Jesus she was doing.

And so the Order was founded.

To own nothing, not a house to live in, not a big convent separating them from the people they served.

Like Jesus, as He teaches in Matthew, they carried nothing for their journey.

Beyond what they needed, they had nothing.

They put on the Holy Habit of Religion.
Now everyone saw who they were and
knew who they could turn to for
sustenance and the lovingkindness of
the Lord Jesus.

They lived at first on the streets with
those they were supporting. Like Jesus,
they had nowhere to lay their heads.

They were not like Nuns from a
Convent, who visited the poor then went
back to their House.

To earn money to feed the homeless
ones, they would gather fruit, anything
that would sell, and sit on the street with
a barrow.

Earning all they gave and giving all they
earned.

Then one day a lady came to them. She
knew the work they did and how poorly
they lived.

She had been left a small cottage, and God told her in a dream to give them this inheritance.

That little, simple House became a House of Grace; the grace of Jesus providing for his Brides.

There the first Sisters lived, twelve in harmony, and from there Sisters over long years went out, two by two, taking nothing, for they had nothing, to parishes throughout the land, and some overseas.

There too Sisters were formed and trained.

From all classes and walks of life.

All this was almost 150 years ago, in the south of England.

And as years and decades passed, the way they lived stayed strong and true.

Always reliant on the work of their hands, and on benefactors. On God providing daily for their needs.

For they were not allowed to own property, or to keep money in the bank, even if they had any.

All went to the very poor and hungry.

As it still does.

They never had any "old money" thus; never any coffers to fall back on.

Wherever they lived, they grew food and worked at whatever they could to earn their keep and feed the hungry.

Determined, loving Jesus and living His teachings.

Prayer always their support and strength.

And always, God met their needs.

So they would see an empty house, that was not needed or used, and ask for it.

Not to own it; but simply to use and care for it.

Sometimes a house they rented would be lent to them; to be used by the Order as long as it existed.

Or used for a set time, say five years, after which they would own it and could sell it if they needed to.

Is that a huge thing to ask?

To use a house, piece of land that is sitting idle?

To live quietly in prayer in a house that no-one needs?

Now these Sisters are in great and urgent need here once more.

Of a quiet place where they can live and use their skills to feed the victims of terrible disasters.

Names like tsunami, Myanmar echo in the heart and will do for many years.

They yearn to do more, but they need here a base, a safe sanctuary.

A refuge where they can live in peace and grow food and emerge from for their work.

They ask nothing more than that, and they would then become invisible – until and unless there is need of their skill and their work.

And then they will respond generously and without stint.

For their original charism stands faithful and true.

It has not changed.

Still dependent on divine providence working through the people of God to reach out in help to the people of God.

Still each and all working every hour they can to feed and clothe Jesus.

Email us on
anchoresscj@yahoo.com

Blessings heap upon you...

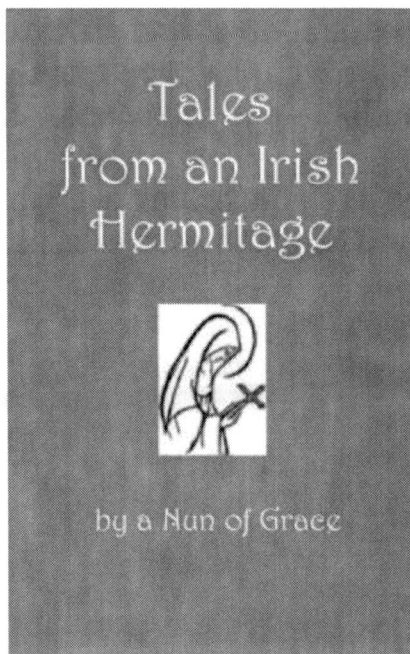

Tales
from an Irish
Hermitage

by a Nun of Grace

A charming collection of tales from
Ireland, where a Nun makes room for
the sheep, hens, geese, and others
nobody else wants.

Order from
www.xanga.com/sistersofgraceofchrist

Or email Sisters of Grace at
anchoresscj@yahoo.com

Tales from an Irish Hermitage
Reviews

"Please keep it a secret, but just about everyone on my gift list will receive a copy of this wonderful book for birthdays and other gifting occasions in the coming year.

"You cannot read from this wonderful little book without a smile on your face and happiness in your heart. These stories about animals can teach us much about ourselves and the humans around us. And I happen to know that each story is the absolute truth.

"Where else can you spend so little, receive so much and do so much good, all at once?

"We can hope for many more volumes in the continuing saga of Sister and the critters."

JA. Texas US

"A few months ago, I was contacted by a nun in Ireland. She was trying to self-publish a book and wondered if I could give her any advice on formatting.

"I already knew her through an online community and had enjoyed her writing very much, so since I had a few weeks of vacation ahead of me, I offered to format the book for her. She sent me the manuscript soon thereafter: *Tales from an Irish Hermitage.*

"This little collection of stories from a tiny hermitage brought me more joy than I anticipated. The author's style is poetic and flowing, meant to be read aloud. Her tales center around the rag-tag animals who come to the hermitage, including an aging ewe named Oonagh, an affectionate gander called Gozzle, and the otherwordly star of 'Seal Magic.' The stories bring together the poignancy of life, the beauty of Ireland, and the understated humour of a unique servant of God.

"This is a book for those who love simple, old-fashioned tales. I am privileged to own the first copy that ever came off the presses, for the Sisters asked me to approve the print work before the book was officially released. It has an honoured place on my shelf, where I will reach for it when my heart wants to be soothed or uplifted.

"I encourage you to purchase a copy as well. All of the proceeds from this book go to help care for homeless children in Sri Lanka, where the Sisters are working in the aftermath of tsunami devastation."

RST, Canada

Seasons
of an Irish
Hermitage

by a Nun of Grace

In the "Irish Hermitage" tradition, this book depicts the passing seasons lived by a Nun on an Irish mountain, in reflections, poems and stories. Easter and Christmas hold their true meaning and beauty, amid the exuberance of flora and fauna cherished at the hermitage.

Order from
www.xanga.com/sistersofgraceofchrist

Or email Sisters of Grace at
anchoresscj@yahoo.com

Seasons of an Irish Hermitage
Reviews

"My initial purchase was twelve books to give as gifts to special people. This book affords us a glimpse into a very different way of life from what most of us live. The stories are delightful, and 100% true. The whole family will enjoy Sister's tales."

"It is a 270 page book of stories, poems and reflections, set, like *Tales from an Irish Hermitage*, in the daily life of a Nun living as a Solitary on an Irish mountain.

"Unmistakably Irish - and unmistakably a book of deep Christian faith and life. Those who know the main anchorhold Web site (http://www.iol.ie/~anchorhold) will recognise reflections they enjoyed there....the poems and stories are new, and the book is rich in graphics.

"This beautifully written book follows on from Tales from an Irish Hermitage, with poetry, reflections, stories and observations of the natural world woven into the framework of the passing year.

"No difficult theories, doctrine or dogma here, just the simple truths of day to day Christian living, loving and giving. An inspiration to all seeking a closer walk with Christ, whether they are living in rural Ireland or in the depths of the city.

"Once read, it is a book to be kept on the bedside table to be dipped into at the end of a difficult day.

"All proceeds go to supporting the work of the Sisters caring for the poorest of the poor, in various parts of the world."

SMG, England

"All the proceeds of sales of this book will go to tend to orphans and the homeless in places around the world. The Nuns can stretch your dollars like you wouldn't believe, but they need the dollars (pounds sterling, euros, etc.).

"This is a charming little book, full of stories, devotions, and prayers. It also

gives a fascinating look into a life that
most of us can hardly imagine.

"It will make a lovely gift for 'the person
who has everything.'"

JA. Texas US

Printed in the United States
142462LV00001B/2/P

9 780980 931723